MOSES

When Harriet Tubman Led Her People to Freedom

Carole Boston Weatherford ❧ Illustrated by Kadir Nelson

 JUMP AT THE SUN

Los Angeles   New York

To the ancestors
who fought for freedom,
and for freedom's children everywhere
—C.B.W.

For my mother, grandmothers,
great-grandmothers, great-greats . . .
and all of the mothers and daughters
who have led the way
—K.N.

Text copyright © 2006 by Carole Boston Weatherford
Illustrations copyright © 2006 by Kadir Nelson

Published by Disney • Jump at the Sun,
an imprint of Disney Book Group

First Edition, September 2006
9 10
H106-9333-5-15024
Printed in Malaysia
Library of Congress Cataloging-in-Publication Data on file.
ISBN 0-7868-5175-9
Visit www.DisneyBooks.com

Reinforced binding
Designed by Ellice M. Lee
This book is set in Kennerley.

FOREWORD

Slavery is a practice in which one person, known as a "master," is allowed through customs or even laws to own another human being. From 1619 to 1865, Africans and their descendants were enslaved in colonial America and the United States. This was the first time in history that enslavement was based solely on skin color. As property, slaves in the United States had no rights. A person born a slave was a slave for life and was forced to work long hours at sometimes dangerous tasks. Slaves who disobeyed could be severely punished. Further, slaves could be sold by one master to another. Such sales often separated slave families forever. Many states forbade slaves to learn to read and write. Slaves had almost no chance of improving themselves or their living conditions.

In 1820, there were about 1.5 million slaves in the United States. By 1861, the slave population had risen to more than 4 million. Slaves were stirred by sermons about the ancient Israelites' journey out of Egypt and drew hope from African American spirituals—songs that sometimes contained coded messages to aid escapes. Somewhere between 40,000 and 100,000 slaves escaped to freedom through a loose network of helpers and hideaways known as the Underground Railroad.

On a summer night, Harriet gazes
at the sky and talks with God.

I am Your child, Lord; yet Master owns me,
drives me like a mule.
Now he means to sell me south in chains to work cotton,
rice, indigo, or sugarcane, never to see my family again.

God speaks in a whip-poor-will's song.

I SET THE NORTH STAR IN
AND I MEAN FOR YOU TO BE

Harriet sees the star twinkling.

My mind is made up. Tomorrow, I flee.

God wraps her in the blanket of night,
and she returns to the cabin,
sleeps beside her husband one last time.

The next day, Harriet tells not a soul her plans.
She grips the ax to chop wood, breathes deeply, and murmurs,

Lord, I'm going to hold steady on to You.

And God whispers back in the breeze,

I'M GOING TO SEE YOU THROUGH, CHILD.

At dusk, Harriet chants,

When *that old chariot comes, I'm going to leave you. . . .*

She hopes her loved ones hear her song
and know it means farewell.
While the plantation sleeps, Harriet prays,

Lord, send me a sign.

Owl screeches.

THE HOUR HAS COME.

Harriet slips into the night.

Running through the swamp, she hears frogs croaking
and her own heart pounding.

Lord, I can't make it alone.

In the moon's reflection on the creek, she sees God's face.

HARRIET, YOU DREAMED THAT SAINTS SAVED YOU, BUT MORTALS WILL GIVE YOU REFUGE.

The woman in the wagon who always spoke kindly to me—

YES, HARRIET—

I must go to her.

The woman points Harriet to safe havens—
hiding places for runaways—
and Harriet steals away into darkness.

She creeps through the woods.
Her heart flutters. Hush: hoofbeats!

*Please, Lord, don't let them catch me and take me back
to face Master's whip. Don't let my journey end here.*

In the underbrush, Harriet sinks into a deep sleep.
God cradles her.
When she wakes, the men on horseback have passed.
And day breaks.

Thank You, Lord, for watching over me.

In a clearing: the safe haven.

Harriet knows that most strangers would turn her in, not help her.

But the farmer's wife feeds Harriet, then tells her to sweep the yard.

I don't know who to trust, Lord.

SEARCH FOR MY FACE IN THEIRS,
AND FOR MY HANDS IN THEIR WORK.
WHAT HAVE YOU IN YOUR HANDS?

In a dust cloud, she sees the broom become a staff,
then a rifle. Harriet startles but holds on.

I WILL ARM YOU AGAINST YOUR ENEMIES,
BUT YOU WILL NOT HARM A SOUL,
AND NO HARM WILL COME TO YOU.

The dust settles as she stops sweeping, and all is as it was.

At nightfall, Harriet climbs into a wagon,
and the farmer covers her with blankets.
As the wagon wobbles along, Harriet worries that it is heading to jail.

Should I leap, Lord?

TRUST ME TO PROTECT YOU, CHILD.

Harriet walks till her legs ache; then she leans against a tree.

Lord, I miss my folks.

HARRIET, YOUR FATHER
TAUGHT YOU TO READ THE STARS,
PREDICT THE WEATHER,
GATHER WILD BERRIES,
AND MAKE CURES FROM ROOTS.

USE HIS LESSONS TO BE FREE.
YOU WILL MEET AGAIN.

A mosquito buzzes in Harriet's ear.
She rises and moves on.

A boatman rows her upriver.

Back on shore, hounds snarl, sniff for Harriet's trail.

She races as fast as she can.

Lord, I can't outrun them.

God speaks through a babbling brook:

SHED YOUR SHOES,

WADE IN THE WATER TO TRICK THE DOGS.

Upstream, the barking ceases
and fear washes away.

Thank You, Lord.

Harriet's feet bleed and her gut churns.
Under the stars, she draws near to God.

Lord, don't let nobody turn me 'round;
I'd rather die than be a slave.

HARRIET, KEEP GOING. YOU HAVE ALREADY GLIMPSED THE FUTURE.

She recalls dreams where she flew like a bird,
sank, and was lifted by ladies in white who pulled her north.

FLY, HARRIET.
YOUR FAITH HAS WINGS.

Up ahead, she hears word that patrollers are nabbing runaways,
and crouches for days in a potato hole,
dreams she is buried alive.

Have You deserted me, Lord?

HARRIET, WHEN YOU WERE A GIRL,
YOU HID IN A PIGPEN TO SHUN
THE WHIP. YOU FOUGHT HOGS
FOR TABLE SCRAPS, ALMOST STARVED
BEFORE YOU FACED THE LASH.
I AM WITH YOU NOW AS I WAS THEN.

An old prayer comes back to her:

Lord, make me strong. Help me fight.

As far as you can walk with Me,

After seven days, Harriet rises from that hole like a sapling,
reaches for the sun as if to touch God's hand.
By moonlight, she marches on,
making her way mile after rugged mile,
hiding in haystacks, attics, and barns,
holding God's hand all the while.
She often wearies.

How far, Lord?

MY CHILD, AND I CAN CARRY YOU.

When Harriet is about to drop, a couple in a wagon ride by.
They say slavery is a sin, and they take her on the last leg of her journey.

NOT FAR NOW, CHILD, NOT FAR NOW.

In the Promised Land, Philadelphia,
the sun shines gold in the trees,
and Harriet feels light as a cloud.
She studies herself from head to toe
to see if she has wings.

Is this heaven, Lord?

NOT HEAVEN, HARRIET, FREE SOIL.

But freedom brings new woes.

Lord, I am a stranger here;
All my kin are down south.

WOULD YOU LIKE TO SEE THEM?

As Harriet dusts, her family's faces

appear in the wood grain.

She wipes a tear from the table.

I would make a home for them here.
I would give my own life to free them.

THEN GO BACK FOR THEM, DAUGHTER.
BUT FIRST, GO TO MY HOUSE
TO PREPARE FOR THE JOURNEY.

And Harriet goes to church,
finds not just holy ground but a stopping place,
a station along the Underground Railroad
that slaves travel to freedom.
Harriet hands out shirts and shoes,
serves butterbeans and biscuits to newly arrived runaways,
while agents who plot escape paths
pass on secret routes that she learns by heart.
Finally a conductor, a guide, she turns to God.

I am ready, Lord. Lead me.

HARRIET, I WILL MAKE A WAY FOR YOU.

Risking her own life, Harriet returns to the dreaded South and rescues her family.
But she dreams of slaves still in the yoke.
She hears their groans, sees their tears, tosses and turns in her sleep.
Then, God opens her eyes.

HARRIET, BE THE MOSES OF YOUR PEOP

But I am a lowly woman, Lord.

HARRIET, I HAVE BLESSED YOU
WITH A STRONG BODY, A CLEVER MIND.
YOU HEAL THE SICK AND SEE THE FUTURE
USE YOUR GIFTS TO BREAK THE CHAINS.

I will do as You say, Lord.
I will show others the way to freedom that You have shown me.

And Harriet heeds God's call,
goes south again and again,
keeps her bands of runaways moving—
come storms and rough country—
clear to Canada: Canaanland.
And when free souls sing her praises,
she gives glory where it is due.

It wasn't me. It was the Lord.
I always trust Him to lead me
and He always does.

WELL DONE, MOSES, WELL DONE.

AUTHOR'S NOTE

This fictional story is based on the spiritual journey of Harriet Tubman—as a slave in Maryland; a free woman in Philadelphia, Pennsylvania; and a famous conductor on the Underground Railroad. Courageous, compassionate, and deeply religious, Tubman saw visions and spoke to God. She believed the Lord called her to free slaves on the Underground Railroad. Her strong faith not only helped her to escape from slavery, but to lead others to freedom.

One of eleven children of Benjamin and Harriet Ross, Tubman was born into slavery around 1820 on a Bucktown, Maryland, plantation. Named Araminta at birth and nicknamed "Minty," Tubman was just seven years old when she was hired out—rented by her master to another household—to care for a baby. She was forced to rock the cradle day and night. When the baby cried, Tubman was whipped.

Eventually, she rebelled against the mistreatment. Once, she ran away and hid in a pigpen for several days to avoid a beating. Another time, after Tubman went to work in the fields, she disobeyed an order to tie up a slave who had escaped. When the slave fled again, the master struck Tubman in the head with a two-pound weight, nearly killing her. For the rest of her life, she bore a scar and suffered severe headaches, blackouts, and fits of speechlessness.

As a young woman, Tubman chopped wood with her father. In the forest, he taught her to gather nuts and berries, make cures from plants and roots, predict the weather, and follow the stars. By adulthood, Tubman had taken her mother's name, Harriet.

In 1844, Harriet's master forced her to marry John Tubman. When her owner died in 1849, she heard that she would be separated from her family and sold south, where slavery was even harsher. Harriet decided to run away, even though her husband refused to go with her and threatened to tell the master. Trusting God, Harriet fled alone on the Underground Railroad, a loosely organized network of safe houses, secret routes, codes and signs, and abolitionists, people who opposed slavery. She journeyed ninety miles, mostly on foot, to Philadelphia, Pennsylvania. Finally free, Harriet felt reborn.

But she worried about her loved ones still enslaved down south. Vowing to free them, she saved the money she earned as a cook and maid. At a church that was an Underground Railroad station, she learned secret routes and the locations of safe houses.

In 1851, Harriet returned to Maryland and led her brothers to freedom. Again and again, she returned to the South, risking her life to free other slaves. Guided by God, she led her bands of runaways hundreds of miles. She talked to God as to a friend and she heeded His commands. In time, she became known as "the Moses of her people." Slave masters offered a forty-thousand-dollar reward for Harriet's capture. To outsmart slave catchers, she took different routes and donned disguises. She used medicine to hush crying babies and threatened to shoot runaways who begged to turn back. In 1857, Harriet carried her aging parents to Canada. By 1860, she had gone south nineteen times and freed as many as three hundred slaves. She never lost a passenger.

Harriet Tubman died in 1913.